D1129762

Dear Boys and Girls:

Crazy Horse was known as the Holy Man, or the Strange Man, of the Oglala Sioux. His father was an Oglala. His mother was a member of my own people, the Brule Sioux.

Oglala and Brule are the names of two divisions of the Dakota Nation. There are many more: the Miniconjou, the Hunkpapa and others. The real name of the Sioux people is Dakota. People usually call us "Sioux" from our Chippewa name, Nadewessiou, which means "Strangers" or "Other People."

Crazy Horse loved his people. He died trying to set them free, like the great patriot that he was. Crazy Horse is still mourned by the Dakota people. In the Black Hills which he loved, a whole mountainside is being carved into a portrait memorial to Crazy Horse.

We can all admire such men and be proud of them.

Sincerely,

Harold Barse

Harold Barse
Brule—Miniconjou Sioux

CRAZY HORSE
SIOUX WARRIOR

BY ENID LaMONTE MEADOWCROFT

ILLUSTRATED BY CARY

GARRARD PUBLISHING COMPANY
CHAMPAIGN, ILLINOIS

To Lisa and Andrea
with love

ALICE MARRIOTT and CAROL K. RACHLIN of Southwest Research Associates are consultants for Garrard Indian Books.

MISS MARRIOTT has lived among the Kiowa and Cheyenne Indians in Oklahoma and spent many years with the Pueblos of New Mexico and the Hopis of Arizona. First woman to take a degree in anthropology from the University of Oklahoma, she is a Fellow of the American Anthropological Association, now working with its Curriculum Project.

MISS RACHLIN, also a Fellow of AAA and of the American Association for the Advancement of Science, is a graduate in anthropology of Columbia University. She has done archaeological work in New Jersey and Indiana, and ethnological field work with Algonquian tribes of the Midwest.

Contents

The Oglalas

Crazy Horse's people—the Oglalas—were of the Sioux family. They were among the most colorful and exciting of all the North American Indians.

The Sioux were warriors and hunters. Dressed in beaded vests, leggings, and bright war feathers, they galloped bareback across the plains.

They chased the herds of wild buffalo, which they needed for food, for clothing and many other uses. And wherever the buffalo went, the Sioux picked up their tepees, their household goods, children, horses and dogs, and followed.

The buffalo meat was sun-dried and kept for months. Some of it was pounded into a meal and mixed with fat and dried berries.

The Sioux were brave, fierce in war, and their name made their enemies shudder. Today, when an Indian is shown in a picture or a design, he is often a member of one of the Plains tribes, like the Sioux.

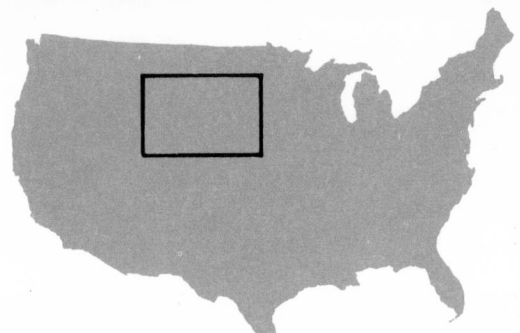

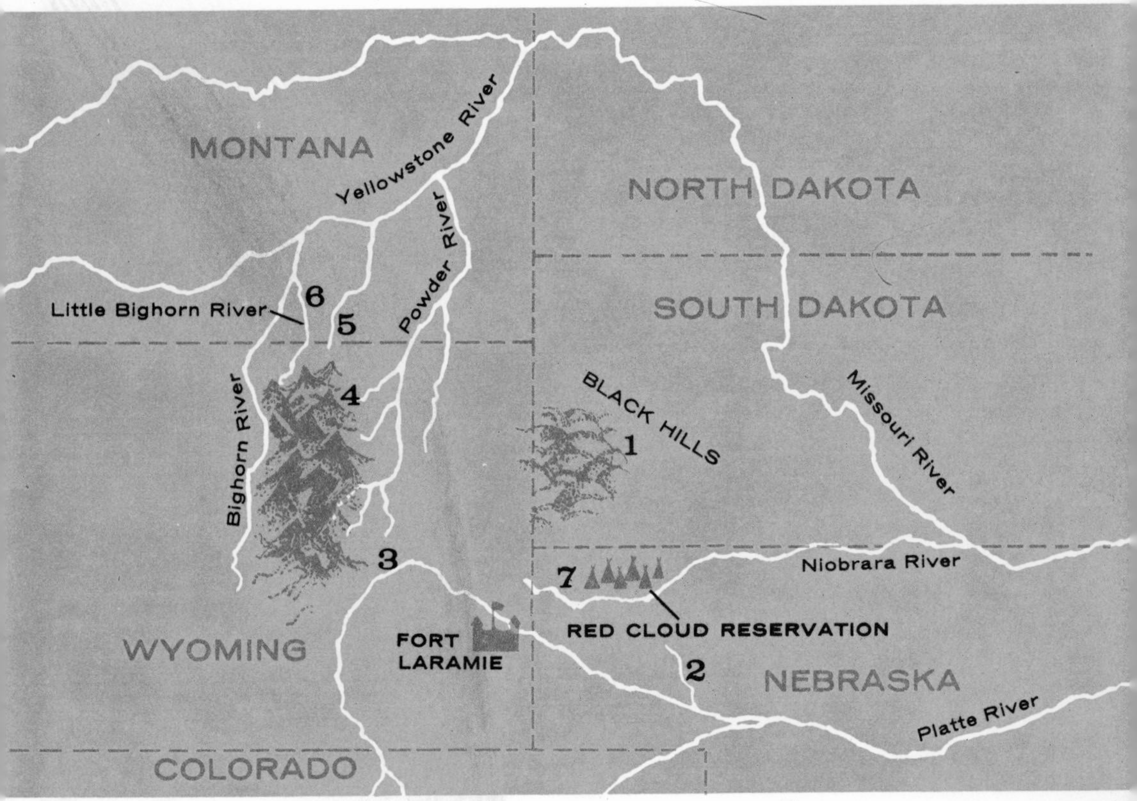

1. Birthplace of Crazy Horse.

2. Blue Water Creek, where Curly found the Indian woman and her child.

3. Platte Bridge, where Crazy Horse led the decoys.

4. The fort attacked by the Sioux in December, 1866.

5. The Battle of the Rosebud, where General Crook was defeated.

6. The Battle of the Little Bighorn, June 25, 1876.

7. Fort Robinson, where Crazy Horse was killed.

1

An Invitation

Curly pulled back hard on his bow-string. He let his arrow fly. It hit a tree and stuck fast. Curly spoke to the tall Indian standing beside him.

"Was that good, Hump?" he asked. "Will I be ready soon to hunt buffalo?"

Hump smiled. "No boy nine winters old can hunt buffalo," he said. "You must wait until you can use a stronger bow. Come, we'll go back to the village now."

Curly pulled his arrow from the tree and followed Hump. He tried to walk through the woods silently, as Hump did.

"When I grow up," he thought, "I want to be called Crazy Horse like my father. But I want to be a warrior like Hump."

Soon he and Hump reached the village. The Oglala Indians were living in a big circle of tepees on the Niobrara River. The Niobrara is in Nebraska. In 1851, when Curly was nine, Nebraska was Indian country. Buffalo roamed over the plains. Wild horses grazed on the hills.

The Oglalas depended on the buffalo for food and hides. They followed the great herds from place to place. When they moved their village they needed many horses. So they caught the wild horses and tamed them. Sometimes they took horses from other tribes.

Curly had his own pony. One day he went off to hunt rabbits. When he came back his sister, Bright Star, ran to meet him.

"There's a meeting at the council tepee," she cried. "Chief Smoke wants to talk to us about the whites. Hurry!"

"The whites!" Curly jumped from his pony.

He had seen white men at their fort.

It was near their road which crossed the Indians' hunting grounds. Curly liked the whites and wanted to hear about them. He ran to the big tepee.

A large crowd had gathered around it. Curly sat down with his mother and his brother, Little Hawk. The sides of the big tepee were rolled up. Inside he could see his father talking with Chief Smoke. Crazy Horse was the Oglalas' holy man and gave them good advice.

At last Smoke stood up.

"A message has come from the white men," he said. "We have all been invited to their fort. Other tribes will be there. The whites want to talk to our chiefs. They will give us all presents. Shall we go?"

"Yes!" cried many of the people.

"No!" cried several of the warriors.

One of them jumped to his feet. "We should have nothing to do with those whites," he shouted. "They give us their white-man sickness. They frighten away our buffalo. We must drive them out before it is too late."

He sat down and everyone began to talk at once. Curly's heart was beating like a drum. Chief Smoke spoke again.

"We have plenty of buffalo," Smoke said quietly. "And there are not many whites. I think we should go to their fort. We should find out why they want to talk to us and give us presents."

"Yes," cried the people. "We will go."

The next morning they took down their tepees and loaded them on their travois. The travois were made of long poles, with nets of rawhide slung between them. One end of the travois was harnessed to a packhorse or a dog. The other end dragged on the ground.

When all the travois were loaded, the Oglalas set out. Five days later they reached Fort Laramie on the Platte River.

Other tribes had already arrived. They all belonged to a big group of tribes called the Sioux. Their tepees and horse herds were spread out far over the plains around Fort Laramie.

Curly was surprised by the number. "I didn't know there were so many of us in all the world," he thought proudly. "Why should any Indians want to drive away a few whites?"

2

Curly Hunts Buffalo

Curly had a good time at Fort Laramie. He and his friends watched the soldiers drill. They raced their ponies along the white-man road. They played war games with boys of other tribes.

One day 27 big wagons rolled into the Indians' great encampment.

"They are bringing the presents from the White Father in Washington," Curly told his friend, Lone Bear. "My father says they were sent because our chiefs signed a promise paper."

"What did they promise?" asked Lone Bear.

"To let the whites build more forts along their road," Curly answered. "And not to hurt white travelers. Then the whites promised to be our friends forever and to give us presents every year for 50 years."

The Indians crowded around the wagons. Soon the presents were handed out. There were hatchets, knives, bolts of red cloth, beads and other things.

Curly's present was a small mirror. It was like the signal mirrors which the warriors used.

Before long the Oglalas returned to their own buffalo country. Then Curly practiced flashing mirror signals in the sun. His father made him a strong, new bow. He practiced with that too.

One evening his father called him into their tepee. Hump was there.

"We've been talking about you, Curly," said his father. "You are ten winters old. It's time you decided what you want to be when you're a man."

"A warrior," Curly replied promptly. "The bravest in the tribe."

Both men smiled. Curly was small for his age. His hair and skin were lighter than those of most Indians. This

made him look weak. But Crazy Horse
and Hump knew that he was strong and
wiry.

"Very well," said his father. "Hump
has offered to train you. But you must
work hard."

"I will work hard," Curly promised.
And he did.

Hump taught him to shoot at a target
while riding on his pony. He trained

Curly to run long distances without stopping to rest. Sometimes Hump made Curly fast for a day and go without water. He gave the boy a wild horse and told him how to tame her.

When Curly was eleven, Hump took him on a big buffalo hunt. Hump led the other hunters. Curly rode beside him. At the top of a hill they stopped.

The plain below them was dark with buffalo. Hump gave a signal.

"Hoka hey!" cried the hunters. "Let's go."

They galloped toward the buffalo. Curly aimed at a calf. His arrow hit a large bull. The animal charged at him. Curly wanted to gallop away, but he sent two more arrows into the bull.

The angry animal still came toward him, faster and faster. Curly shot again. The bull sank to the ground and died.

The other hunters killed many buffalo. That night there was a feast in the village. Then some of the warriors walked around the big circle of tepees. Each one sang of a brave deed he had done that day. Hump sang about Curly.

"On his first hunt," sang Hump, "he

bravely killed an angry bull. Let us call out his name."

"Curly! Curly!" called the people. "Stand out where we can see you."

But Curly sat hidden in the shadow of his father's tepee. "It is not much to kill a buffalo," he thought. "Some day I must do things which are braver still."

3

A Runaway Cow

The Oglalas went twice to Fort Laramie to get their presents. The third time they went the presents did not come. They waited many days. So did other Sioux Indians.

Curly did not like waiting. He wanted to get back to the buffalo country. One hot day he stood by the white-man road, watching a wagon train roll by. A white man walked behind the wagons driving an old cow.

Suddenly five boys from the Brule tribe came racing toward the road. Each tried to reach it first. They yelled and whipped up their ponies.

The noise frightened the cow. She bolted into the Brule village. Darting into a tepee, she came out with a bundle stuck on her horns.

Curly and the Brule boys chased her, shouting with glee. On the cow ran, knocking over a kettle of stew, and kicking up a big cloud of dust.

Dogs barked. Men laughed. Women

and children scrambled out of her way.

"Shoot her," cried an old woman. "She'll hurt someone."

A warrior named Straight Foretop quickly shot the cow. The owner of the cow hurried to Fort Laramie. He reported that the Indians had stolen his cow and killed her.

Soon bad news reached the Indians. Soldiers were coming from the fort to arrest Straight Foretop and put him in jail.

"For shooting a *cow*!" Curly could not believe it. To take away an Indian's freedom was a terrible punishment. Nothing could be worse.

"No whites will ever lock *me* up in a box with iron bars," Curly said to Lone Bear. "I'd kill anyone who tried."

The boys waited outside the Brule village, watching for the soldiers. They came at last, led by an officer named Grattan.

Grattan did not like Indians. He could not speak their language. So he had brought an interpreter named Wyuse. Wyuse was drunk.

The village seemed empty. Not an

Indian was in sight. Wyuse galloped around the circle of tepees.

"Come out, you red devils," he yelled. "We'll kill you like dogs."

Chief Conquering Bear stepped from his tepee. He walked bravely toward Grattan.

"Don't hurt my people," he said quietly. "We can settle this matter

peacefully, my friend. We will give you five fine horses to pay for that cow."

The chief waited for Wyuse to put his words into white-man language. No one knows what Wyuse said. Suddenly Grattan shouted an order. His soldiers raised their guns and shot Conquering Bear.

Instantly the village was filled with angry warriors. Grattan and his men tried to flee. But the warriors chased them and killed every one.

Curly had never seen men killed before. It made him feel sick and not at all brave.

The Indians did not want more trouble with any whites. They packed up their tepees. By nightfall they were heading for the hills.

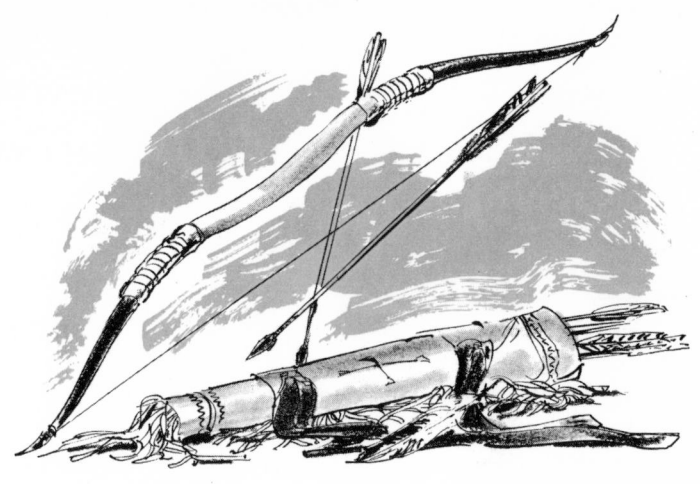

4

"I Hate the Whites"

Curly's mother was a Brule Indian. She missed her own people. So Curly's family traveled with the Brules for a while. The Brules set up their tepees on Blue Water Creek. It was a long way from Fort Laramie.

Curly missed Hump, but he was happy. A year passed. Then a terrible thing happened.

Soldiers from the fort came to punish the Brules for killing Grattan and his men. They surprised the peaceful village. The warriors had no time to arm themselves. Many men, women and children were killed. Others were carried off to the jail at Fort Laramie.

Curly was away that day, hunting in the sand hills. In the evening he rode home. There he saw the bodies on the ground. Curly looked swiftly for his father and mother, for Little Hawk and Bright Star. They were not there.

Then he saw moccasin tracks leading north, and he knew that some Indians had escaped. He followed the tracks.

Suddenly he heard a woman crying. He found her hiding in some bushes, holding a tiny baby.

"They have killed my husband," she sobbed, "and my little boy. I am too sick to walk, too sick to ride. So I will die here with my baby."

"No," said Curly "I'll help you."

He had seen a broken travois on the trail. He ran back to get it and hitched it to his horse. Carefully he put the woman onto it. Then he went on, leading his horse.

The moon shone dimly. All night he followed the tracks of the fleeing Indians. At dawn he found the people, camping beside a lake. His family was there, caring for the wounded. Little Hawk told him about the attack.

Curly grew hot with anger as he listened. He remembered the women and children he had seen, lying dead on the ground. He thought of the people who had been carried off to jail. He remembered the shooting of brave Conquering Bear.

"Why do they do these terrible things to us?" he cried. "I hate the whites! I hate them!"

He hoped that some warriors would rescue the people in the fort jail. But the Brules were not strong enough now to send out a war party against the whites. When the wounded could travel, they all moved farther north.

Curly and his family stayed with them for nearly two years. Then they went to live again with the Oglalas.

5

Curly Wins His Name

The Oglalas were living near the Powder River in Montana. Curly was glad to be with them again.

One morning he saw Hump and other warriors putting on war paint and feathers.

"Where are you going?" he asked Hump. "Against an enemy tribe?"

"Yes," said Hump. "It's a strange tribe. They are grass-house people. They have many horses. We're going to take some."

"Please take me with you," Curly said quickly. "Please."

Hump looked him over. Curly was seventeen now. He was still small for his age. But he had worked hard to learn all that a good warrior should know.

"All right," said Hump. "Get your weapons."

Curly ran for his bow and arrows and his horse. His heart pounded with excitement. This was his first war party.

The grass-house warriors knew the

Oglalas were coming. Their scouts had told them. They were waiting on a high hill, behind large rocks. Many of them had guns.

Some of the Oglalas had guns too. They circled the hill, whooping and shooting. Then they tried to ride to the top. But the enemy drove them back. Finally the Oglalas gathered some

distance away to plan their next move.

Suddenly Curly left them. He galloped toward the hill and straight up the side. Bullets and arrows flew all around him. Still he rode on.

A grass-house warrior rose from a gully and aimed a gun at his head. Curly shot him quickly. Whirling around, he killed another warrior who was sneaking up behind him.

The Oglalas below sent up a great cheer. Curly slid from his horse and scalped the dead men. More bullets flew around him. An arrow hit him in the leg. He looked for his horse. The animal had bolted. Limping badly, Curly scrambled down the hill.

Hump met him with another horse. They rode away from the fighting. Hump cut the arrow from Curly's leg.

"You did well," he said. "While you kept the enemy busy, our men took some fine horses. Now you are a warrior. I'm proud of you."

Curly smiled. Although his leg hurt badly, he was happy.

That night the Oglalas had a big celebration. The warriors danced around the village campfire. Each one told of

a brave deed he had done that day. Then it was Curly's turn. But he could not talk about himself before so many people.

So his father stepped into the firelight, wrapped in his holy blanket. He walked slowly around the circle, singing,

"Today, my son has fought bravely against a strange tribe.

"He has become a man and earned a man's name.

"I give him the great name my father gave to me.

"I give him the name Crazy Horse."

The people fell into line behind him. Together they chanted the name of their brave new warrior.

"Crazy Horse! Crazy Horse! Crazy Horse!"

6

A Brave Decoy

Six years passed. The Oglalas stayed in the Powder River country. They had more fights with enemy tribes. Young Crazy Horse became one of their bravest warriors.

Meanwhile, Indians to the south were having trouble with the whites. Many settlers and soldiers had moved into their country near the Platte River. Most of the whites treated the Indians badly. They were afraid of them.

"The only good Indian is a dead Indian," they said.

Sometimes they killed Indians who were their friends. Early one morning 700 soldiers attacked a village of peaceful Cheyenne Indians. It was a surprise attack. Most of the Cheyennes were killed. Only a few escaped.

Runners quickly carried the news to the Powder River country. In every Sioux village, angry warriors gathered up their weapons. Then they rode south to punish the whites.

On a hot July morning a large war party rode quietly toward a fort on the Platte River. Hump was leading it. Crazy Horse was one of the decoys.

Two miles from the fort the warriors reached some sand hills.

"Hide in these hills," Hump told them. "Our brave decoys will go to the fort. They'll trick the soldiers into coming out and lead them back here. When the soldiers are close enough, I'll give a signal. Then you must all rush out together and surround them."

The warriors hid. Crazy Horse and three other decoys rode on. Some mules were grazing near the fort. The decoys pretended that they were going to steal them. A sentry shouted. The fort gates swung open. Out rode 60 soldiers.

They fired at the decoys and chased them part way to the sand hills. Crazy Horse saw them start to turn back.

Quickly he slid from his horse. Crouching down, he examined her foot. He pretended it was hurt. With a shout the soldiers rode toward him. He leaped into his saddle and galloped ahead.

Bullets whistled past his ears. The soldiers were close behind him. He led them nearer to the sand hills. Soon they were almost near enough to be trapped.

But suddenly some of the warriors broke out of hiding. With shrill war cries they rushed at the enemy. The soldiers turned swiftly and galloped safely back to the fort.

Crazy Horse was hot with anger.

"You are like children," he shouted

at the warriors. "Each of you wants to prove how brave he is. So you won't wait for your signal. The whites wait. They obey orders. They fight together. That's why they're strong."

Some of the warriors laughed at this. But the rest were ashamed. The next day the brave decoys lured the soldiers from the fort with another trick. This time the warriors waited. They rushed out from their hiding places together and most of the soldiers were killed.

"It is good to listen to Crazy Horse," the warriors agreed. "He is wise."

The Oglala chiefs were pleased with Crazy Horse, too. They gave him a beautiful beaded shirt and a fine new horse. They told him that he was now a leader of the tribe.

7

Crazy Horse
Is Doubtful

White men soon pushed right into the
Powder River country. They wanted to
dig for gold in the Big Horn Mountains.

Miners' wagons rattled along the trail
to the mountains, scaring the buffalo.
Soldiers built a fort near the river.

In December of 1866, many Sioux warriors banded together to attack the fort. Crazy Horse led the decoys. Before the attack he spoke to the warriors. He reminded them of what had happened at the fort near the Platte.

"This is a larger fort," he said. "There are many more soldiers to be trapped. I'll wave a blanket over my head when it's time for you to break out of hiding. Wait for that signal, or all will be spoiled."

"We'll wait," the warriors promised. And they did.

The battle was a fierce one. Though the soldiers fought bravely, many were killed. But this did not discourage the whites.

"They are running over our land like ants," Crazy Horse said to his father one day in spring. "If we don't stop the whites now, more will come, and more and more."

He painted a yellow streak on his cheek and stuck a feather in his hair. Then he picked up his weapons and strode from the tepee. Soon he was leading a large war party toward the Bozeman Trail.

Sitting Bull and Red Cloud, leaders of other Sioux tribes, also led warriors against the whites. The Indians attacked wagon trains and stagecoaches. They burned miners' shacks. They stole horses and cattle. They killed travelers. No white man felt safe.

One warm summer day an Indian who was friendly to the whites rode into the Oglalas' village. He brought them a message from the soldiers at Fort Laramie.

"The whites are tired of fighting," he told the Oglalas. "If you will stop it, they will give you fine presents."

"We don't want presents," cried Crazy Horse angrily. "We want the whites to get out of our country. Tell them we'll fight until they do."

Other Sioux leaders sent the same message. So the whites decided to give up. On a morning in August, 1867, the soldiers left the fort. Sitting quietly on their horses, hundreds of warriors watched them ride away. Then joyfully, the warriors set fire to the fort and burned it to the ground.

The Sioux had won a big victory. The Oglalas sent Chief Red Cloud to Fort Laramie to put his mark on a peace treaty with the whites. He was proud and happy when he returned.

"The whites have promised to stay out of the Powder River country forever," he announced. "And they have promised that as long as grass grows and water flows, the country shall be ours."

Crazy Horse smiled doubtfully. He wondered how long the whites would keep their promise.

8

Chief Crazy Horse

Crazy Horse was glad that he could stop fighting whites. Now he was free to do other things. Before long he married a fine young woman named Black Shawl. A baby daughter was born to them and for nearly four years they were happy.

Then their little girl died of the white man's coughing disease. And soon after that, the whites broke their promise.

Again miners and soldiers streamed into the Powder River country. This time they were after gold in the Black Hills. Crazy Horse led many war parties out to drive them away. But the whites came on like a flood.

Soon an Indian messenger from Fort Laramie rode into the Oglala village.

"The White Father in Washington wants to buy the Black Hills," he told the Oglalas.

"We won't sell them," replied Crazy Horse quietly. "The Great Spirit gave them to us to keep."

Another messenger went to talk to Sitting Bull. He also refused to sell the hills. But Chief Red Cloud agreed to sell if he could get a good price. So did another chief named Spotted Tail.

Crazy Horse could not understand these two leaders. They had grown friendly with the whites. Now they were living with their people on reservations near Fort Laramie.

On the reservations they had to obey white soldiers. They had to eat food given to them by whites. They could not hunt buffalo without permission. They could no longer roam where they pleased.

"A reservation is like a jail without walls," Crazy Horse said to Black Shawl. "I'll never live in a jail. I'd rather die."

Black Shawl nodded and choked back

a cough. She, too, had caught the white man's terrible coughing sickness. When winter came her cough grew worse.

Crazy Horse hated to leave her. But he had to lead war parties against the miners. One snowy night he returned late to the village. A friend rode to meet him.

"A man from Fort Laramie came today," he said. "The whites are angry because we won't sell the hills. Now they say that all Indians must move out of the Powder River country. We must go to the reservations near the fort. If we don't go soon, they will send a big army against us. What shall we do?"

"We'll fight for our country," said Crazy Horse promptly.

He knew that Sitting Bull would decide to fight too.

"Our people will be stronger if we're together," he thought.

So he led the Oglalas north to Sitting Bull's camp. It was in the valley near the Rosebud River.

Through the winter other Indians joined them there. In the spring their leaders met to choose a war chief. An Oglala named Big Road stood up in the council lodge.

"Crazy Horse is strong and wise in battle," he said. "In the village he is generous and kind. He shares his meat and horses with the poor. He will always do what is best for the people. Let us make him our war chief for the rest of his life."

"*Hou!*" cried the people around the council tepee. "Crazy Horse will be our war chief. Crazy Horse! Crazy Horse!"

They crowded closer to watch him take his turn at smoking the chief's pipe. When he left the lodge they lifted him to the back of a handsome white warhorse. Then they followed him around

the great encampment, joyfully shouting his name.

This was the spring of 1876. Crazy Horse was 33 years old.

"I do not yet have enough wisdom to be a powerful war chief," he thought. "But I will pray to the Great Spirit to help me and do the best I can."

9

"Be Strong. Follow Me".

"A big war is coming against the whites. Crazy Horse is our war chief. He will lead us. Come and fight."

Runners carried this message to the reservations near Fort Laramie. Many Indians on the reservations wanted to follow Crazy Horse. They stole away at night with their families and hurried north.

The camp in the valley of the Rosebud grew larger every day. The people enjoyed being together. They seemed to forget about the white men. But Crazy Horse and Sitting Bull did not forget. Their scouts were out day and night, watching for the enemy.

One June evening Crazy Horse heard a sound in the distance like a wolf howling. It was a scout signaling danger. Crazy Horse called all the people to the council lodge. The scout arrived and spoke to them.

"The Rosebud is black with soldiers," he said. "Three Stars leads them. They are only one sleep away."

"*Hoppo!*" cried a warrior. "Let's go and fight them."

"No!" shouted another. "Wait here

for them. We must stay to protect the helpless ones."

Now everyone began to talk at once. The old chiefs did not know what to do. Then Crazy Horse stood up.

"Some warriors will stay here to protect our women and children," he said. "I will lead the others against the whites. Their army is large and very strong. But if we fight together, we can win. All who are coming with me, get ready."

Nearly a thousand warriors hurried to get weapons and horses. An hour later they set out with Crazy Horse.

They traveled all night. Early in the morning they reached a ridge of hills near the Rosebud River. The warriors rode quietly to the top. There below them was the camp of General Crook, whom the Indians called Three Stars.

His soldiers did not know the Indians were near. Then one of Crook's scouts shouted an alarm. The soldiers ran for their guns and horses. Down the ridge rode the warriors. And the fight began.

The Sioux fought fiercely. So did the whites. Once some warriors fell back before the whites' far-shooting guns. Crazy Horse rode quickly to stop them.

"Stand fast!" he cried. "Remember the helpless ones at home! Be strong! Follow me!"

Boldly he rode toward the enemy. The warriors followed him and the fighting began again. The battle lasted almost all day. Finally the whites gave up. They retreated toward the south.

Crazy Horse and his warriors did not go after them. They had no bullets left and only a few arrows. Eight Indians had been killed and some others were wounded. The warriors put the dead and the wounded in travois. Then they started slowly back to the encampment.

They had won a big victory. But Crazy Horse could not rejoice. He felt sure there would soon be more fighting. Two days later, he and Sitting Bull led all their people farther to the north.

10

Terrible Times

The Indians set up their tepees along the Little Bighorn River in Montana. There was good grass for the horses. The hunters brought in plenty of meat. Five days passed peacefully.

On the next day—June 25, 1876—the morning was hot. Children splashed in the river. Women worked at their easiest tasks. Men loafed in the shade.

Suddenly a scout galloped into the encampment.

"Soldiers coming!" he cried. "Many soldiers!"

At once the camp was filled with confusion. Women called their children. They grabbed their babies and fled to the hills. Boys raced to drive in the horses. Warriors ran for their weapons. Each man seized the first horse that came along and rode out to meet the soldiers.

Crazy Horse lined them up.

"Be strong!" he shouted. "Fight together! *Hoka hey!*"

The soldiers were shooting into the camp. Suddenly Crazy Horse gave a signal. With wild war cries the warriors charged. Slowly the soldiers fell back. Most of them were shot down. The rest fled. Then there was another alarm.

"More soldiers! Down the river! On the other side!"

"This is a good day to die!" cried Crazy Horse. *"Follow me!"*

Waving his rifle over his head, he galloped down the riverbank. Whooping warriors raced after him. Sitting Bull was leading warriors too. Whipping up their horses, they all crossed the river.

On came the soldiers. They were led by General Custer, whom the Indians called Yellow Hair. After a hard fight, the Indians surrounded them. Custer

and his men fought bravely. But when the battle ended every one of them was dead.

Many Indians had been killed or wounded. There was weeping in the camp that night. The next day scouts signaled that more soldiers were coming with cannon.

Crazy Horse knew that the warriors could not fight again so soon. Quickly the Indians loaded their travois and started north. Before long Crazy Horse and Sitting Bull decided to separate.

"That will make it harder for the soldiers to find us," they told their people.

So the great Sioux encampment was broken up. Each tribe went its own way. But wherever the Indians went, the soldiers tracked them down. There was more fighting. The noise of battle drove many buffalo away.

Winter came. It was bitter cold. The Indians did not have enough meat. They needed hides for new tepees and robes.

Now and then messengers from Fort Laramie rode into the Oglalas' village.

"Come to Red Cloud Reservation," they said. "The whites will give you blankets and plenty of food. They will give you new tents. Surrender and come to Red Cloud."

"And lose our freedom!" Crazy Horse answered angrily. "No!"

Weeks passed and things grew worse. Sitting Bull's people fled to Canada to escape from the soldiers. But the

Oglalas could not travel so far. They had no ammunition, and many were sick.

Often Crazy Horse left the village. Alone on the top of a little hill, he talked to the Great Spirit.

"Help me plan for my people," he begged. "Show me how to save them."

One spring evening he walked into his tepee and spoke to Black Shawl.

"I have hated the whites ever since they shot Conquering Bear," he said quietly. "I'd rather die than surrender to them. But, to save my people, I must lead them to Red Cloud."

11

A Sad Ending

In May the Oglalas went to Red Cloud. A large crowd of whites waited at Fort Robinson near the reservation to watch them arrive.

Crazy Horse led the long procession. He rode past the whites on his big war-horse, looking straight ahead.

At the reservation all the Indians dismounted. Soldiers took away their horses and weapons. The women put up the tepees. And the wild, free life of the Oglalas was ended.

Crazy Horse made sure they were all given food. Then he went to his own tepee. He was worried about Black Shawl. Her cough was so bad he was afraid she might die. Her people lived on the Spotted Tail Reservation and she wanted to see them. So they set out together early in September.

Crazy Horse did not have permission to leave. The officers at Fort Robinson were afraid he'd stir up the Spotted Tail Indians. "He'll get them to join our Oglalas," one said, "and lead them against us. We must stop him."

Scouts were sent at once to catch Crazy Horse and arrest him. But he and his wife reached Spotted Tail safely. An officer named Lee met them. Crazy Horse explained why they had come.

"Your wife may stay," said Major Lee. "But you must go back tomorrow. You may tell the general at Fort Robinson what you've told me. No harm will come to you."

"That is good," said Crazy Horse wearily. "I don't want to make trouble. I only want peace."

The next day he was taken to Fort Robinson. The general would not see him. Another officer shook his hand.

"Come with me," he said. "I'll show you where to spend the night."

Crazy Horse walked quietly with him

past some armed guards and through a door. Suddenly he jumped back. Ahead of him was what he hated most—a white-man jail! Whirling around, he pulled out his knife. Guards grabbed his arms.

"Let me go!" he cried, fighting with all his might to get away. "Let me go!"

"Kill him!" shouted the officer.

A soldier with a bayonet lunged toward Crazy Horse and stabbed him in the back. The great war chief staggered and sank to the ground. Before morning he was dead.

He had fought bravely to hold his country and to keep his people free. He lost the fight. But today Americans speak of him proudly and remember the name of a great leader—Crazy Horse.